THE RINGMASTER'S APPRENTICE

Oz Hardwick was born in Plymouth, 1960. He is the author of five previous collections of poetry, and editor of *Truths and Disguises* (bluechrome, 2005) and *Subterranean Homesick Yorkshire Blues* (Indigo Dreams, 2008). He is also a photographer and musician, and a professor of Creative Writing at Leeds Trinity University. He lives in York.

The Ringmaster's Apprentice

Oz Hardwick

Valley Press

for Janet, Melissa & Robin
for the warm welcome,
and for S.E. and Gay
for the welcome & the jam

First published in 2014 by Valley Press
Woodend, The Crescent, Scarborough, YO11 2PW
www.valleypressuk.com

First edition, first printing (September 2014)

ISBN 978-1-908853-43-1
Cat. no. VP0058

Text and cover photograph © Oz Hardwick 2014

The right of Oz Hardwick to be identified as the
author of this work has been asserted in accordance with
the Copyright, Designs and Patents Act 1988.

All rights reserved. No part of this publication may be
reproduced, stored in or introduced into a retrieval system,
or transmitted in any form, by any means (electronic,
mechanical, photocopying, recording or otherwise) without
prior written permission from the rights holders.

A CIP record for this book is available from the British Library.

Printed and bound in Great Britain by
Imprint Digital, Upton Pyne, Exeter

www.valleypressuk.com/authors/ozhardwick

Contents

A Train and a Fox 9
Interruption at the Bus Depot 10
Immigration 11
Roadside 12
The Collector 13
California on the 'L' 14
Beatrice on the Northern Line 15
Cornucopia 16
Sacrifice 17
Beneath the Bridge 18
The Secret Library 19
Woman with an Umbrella 20
Gaslight 21
The Ghosts of Liverpool 8 22
Kid Auto on the M25 23
No Smoke 24
Armada 25
Afterglow 26
Sleeping with Dragons 27
Falcon 28
The Alchemist's Cat 31
Toad Stone 32
A Tiding of Magpies 33
The Ringmaster's Apprentice 34
A Word to St George 36
Moon Ballet 37
In the Waiting Room 38
Intensive Care 39
If I Were You 40
Arches 41

Monument 42
The Demolition Men 1960 43
A Rock'n'Roll Tour of Plymouth 44
Vinyl Junkie 46
Bound for Glory 47
Elvis Lives Next Door 48
Bad 49
Asylum 50
Statte Station 51
while we slept 52
Passing Over 53

Acknowledgements

Thanks are due to the editors of the following magazines, periodicals and anthologies, in which some of these poems first appeared: *Along the Iron Veins* (Stairwell Books), *Balancing Act* (Leaf Books), *Bestiario* (Wyvern Works), *Bite Me, Robot Boy* (Dog Horn Publishing), *CC&D*, *The Connecticut Review*, *The Dawn Treader*, *The Eclectic Eel*, *Heart Shoots* (Indigo Dreams Press), *HQ*, *Indigo Rising*, *Inky Squib*, *The Interpreter's House*, *Iota*, *The Iron Book of New Humorous Verse* (Iron Press), *Literary Town Hall* (SCARS Publications), *Lone Stars*, *The Morning Star*, *The Night Light*, *Orbis*, *Reach*, *Reflections on Lake Orta* (Wyvern Works), *Roundtable Review*, *SCARS Poetry Calendar* (SCARS Publications), *Sentinel Champions*, *Sentinel Literary Quarterly*, *The Slab* and *When the Tramp Met the King* (Ek Zuban Press).

A Train and a Fox

This is not Adlestrop – you'd be hard pressed
to romanticise this unscheduled stop by York
Sewage Treatment Works. The scent of grubby grass
is overpowered by a chemical stench
worse than the stink it masks.

The Class 144 Pacer fails
to add that touch of nostalgic steam –
it's simply inconvenient at the end
of a long day. There are no announcements
as 'customers' fidget and hiss into mobiles.

Then, from out of the scrub by the grey fence –
a fox. Make no mistake, he is not Reynard
or Chaucer's Daun Russell. At best
he is *vulpes vulpes*, but won't answer to that either,
nor will he escape the gallows, nor even talk.

No, as a living, breathing fox, he will not consider
narrative, metaphor, or abstract symbol. Yet,
before resuming his animal business, our eyes meet
and, between a bland train and an unconcerned fox,
hangs more poetry than I will ever write.

Interruption at the Bus Depot

Their hair is too neat, their faces too perfect
to recognise. They are invisible until they suddenly
materialise at your shoulder. Their clothes match,
a uniform anonymity, a quintessence of the crowd
from which they appear. *Come with us.*

You try to turn, but they hold you without
touching. You try to speak but cannot
recognise the sounds that stumble, incoherent,
from your dry mouth. They appear amused
but impatient. They are insistent. *Come with us.*

Your vision blurs, you cannot read
identity cards as you try to explain
you have somewhere to be, you are already late,
people are waiting. It's important. *No*,
they say – and it's true. *Come with us.*

Immigration

In the airport, strangers are wearing masks. Security
scans scared eyes, prints fingers,
asks awkward questions. Barefoot queues
do not move. Time passes. It seems
nobody in America speaks English. Dogs
sniff old air in the New World. Everything

looks the same. The same thin girl,
maybe Hispanic or central European,
waits at tables, doesn't look old enough
to have been here so long. She brings Mexican food,
local beer, a glass clouded with cold,
an air of resigned sadness. She has waited here

since her first ancestors came, wiping tables
until she sees her face reflected. Perfect. Masked
strangers fill the halls, the shops, the bars,
throng moving walkways, but she and I
have always been here, speaking the same language
of simple needs. Welcome to the Land of the Free.

Roadside

A smoky bar: all the world's here
in small measures, inscrutable strangers
blank behind neat labels. Svedka Vanilla?
No thanks. Buffalo Trace sounds worse.
Last time I saw something the colour of Bombay Saphire
it was in a lamp during the Winter of Discontent.

The staff look like athletes – football or beach volleyball,
depending. Cigarettes carry no warnings:
Master-crafted blend of only the finest
hand-picked Turkish, like Bogart smoked,
looking cool before he discovered cancer.
The TV shows adverts with the sound turned down.

It's some highway that led me here, straight
and empty, barrelling rain-blind through ghost towns,
chasing the white line from night to night
to drink alone in a small-town cheap hotel.
How far are we from Chicago? asks a woman at the bar.
Half way, answers the barman, not looking.

The Collector

I woke in the carriage, still counting trees
passing, the night before, almost close enough
to touch sickly leaves. I half remembered
hesitant but precise English, awkwardly accented
as she spoke of burning witches outside the gates
of old cities whose names she could not recall.

Her skin was pale, dry as parchment, blue
eyes too watery for ink. She tried to explain
that stories grow off the edge of maps, as language
becomes uncomfortable, uneasy in tight mouths.

She lost all words, became silent
as I counted passing trees, measuring my course

from one unfixed point to another.

California on the 'L'

Doors open in California and everyone's sleeping:
the Chinese woman, head held like the moon,

caught in sidelight beneath a sign that reads
Forest; matching Italians with eyes open

behind Mafia glasses; a scar-faced preacher
in outsized trainers, murmuring blessings or curses

on us all; a heavily elegant black woman,
phone embossing her cheek, lips smudged

against her wrist; a skinny Puerto-Rican kid
in a shirt that says *England*. But this is California

and we're all in other places, soliciting and gambling
are prohibited, so we sleep in silence, punctuated

by the whisper of doors closing.

Beatrice on the Northern Line

Between light and dark, the quick and the still,
she came for me. Star-bright and shadow, steady
voice without sound, eyes speaking, silence
crackled electric. She reached to touch,
without moving, and spoke:

Friend. Lover. Enemy
of Fortune: keep your silver
dark; keep your heart
pure; keep your back
turned from darkness.
I have travelled far: do not
follow. Do not   follow.

Under the earth, dog-tied
twisting fragments, roots
beneath gallows, fruit gripped
tight in sweating palms:
no sleep –
        just the mill
and wrench, a tearing
without end. Until:

Star-bright and shadow, silent,
d^a_escending.

Cornucopia

Midday. Cats stretch beneath benches,
striped by sharp-edged shadows. Sleep.
As grass gasps between worn stones,
the empty church, laced with ribbons,
plucks bleached sky into colour.

Listen. Out from the song of the sighing sea,
rings on her fingers, rings in her ears,
the surf-crowned, gull-eyed, jewelled muse
with servants bearing fruit and flowers,
whispers her song to empty streets.

Proud and benign, she leads her band
of silent brass and strings, twisting
between shuttered shops and boarded cafes,
stirring no dust, bestowing quiet
blessings on bright whitewashed thresholds.

Come, she whispers, *come and enter,*
tread the maze that knows no end.
And I can only follow, smiling
through pathways, where murmured words
seep through walls, soothing and promising.

Somewhere off ahead, around this corner,
or maybe the next, a young girl sits,
absorbed, intent, reading glass poems
beneath unnecessary chandeliers, silently
mouthing words by her own light.

Sacrifice

Young men heft statues in the heavy heat,
thin linen stained with sweat at their backs.
Slicked hair holds bright petals,
at odds with taut faces, wincing
at the weight and the bite of stone into feet.
They no longer hear the crowd, crushed
about them, nor feel its swell and sway.
Fine ash from spent fireworks
drifts gently onto infinite time, measured
in steps and the weight of their fathers' religion.

Later, they will piss on their blisters. A world away,
at the empty church, veil-swathed women carry flowers,
sweep the steps, stare into the dark interior
as children cast petals to the wind.

Beneath the Bridge

Without distance there is no need for bridges
passing through space, like loose tongues linking
souls that never touch, except
through the hard language of wood, steel, stone.

I wait in darkness beneath the bridge, alone,
hungrily anticipating your passage,
head high, tasting the succulent sky,
oblivious to my stunted mumbling deep below.

Your feet tap tattoos, unintelligible codes
of families, friends, careless close connections,
easy freedoms I'll never understand.
All your steps say: *I don't know you.*

Disconnected, my stifled speech
wordlessly proclaims: *I will eat you for my supper.*

The Secret Library

Words hide behind a bland façade, carefully
arranged in codes of whim and chance, secret ciphers
for those in the know, as store fronts stand guard, distracting
prying eyes before blending into the Saturday crowd, arousing
no suspicion, and plain-clothes librarians smuggle lines
through edgy customers, creep unseen up the back stairs
to sink into leather armchairs, surrounded by books and silence.

Out in the street, frustrated car horns blare, irate
parents berate impatient children, and a homeless loner
raises his head to a sound like turning pages, distant
thunder, flowers falling hard from the cloudless sky.

Woman with an Umbrella

after John Atkinson Grimshaw

At nightfall she is there, still in pools of moonlight,
gaslight – a twilight glow silhouetting her dark
profile. Gazing away, she is caught in motion,
looking for something, someone we cannot know,
lost in layers of forgetfulness. In the languishing city,
by the cold quayside, she half turns, pauses,
perhaps believes for a moment she sees, but
no. So, from the tired heart of London
to grimy northern ports and far beyond,
we will always see her, rooted to slick stone
as bare branches, skeletal spars, scratch
at liquid sky, clawing down moonlight
as she stops, drenched in reflection, transfixed by nothing.

Gaslight

In the shadow of the fallen star, the end of the rainbow,
the kissed stone, we turn our collars to sideways sleet.
This is not Chicago, but Yorkshire, and, when I take off
my glasses, all edges will blur but I will still be ugly.
I used to work in a bookshop, she says, *but it closed.*
In the cellar, girls in lace caps washed dead babies
by fat candlelight. I'm not listening. It's only words,
like salt on chapped lips, colours smudging back to grey
and the cold wind snapping between here and nothing.

The Ghosts of Liverpool 8

The ghosts of Liverpool 8 still smoke
in public places, plan their moves
on antique maps, whistle loudly
in the new cathedral which echoes when they've gone.

They ride their bicycles down crowded pavements,
saddlebags stuffed with smuggled words
from Ireland, America, La-la Land,
to trade for songs at late-night lock-ins,
where they crash the party, laugh in italics,
read poems from beer mats and fag packets,
spill drinks, embarrass their friends,
smile and leave with the prettiest girls.

The ghosts of Liverpool 8 never sleep,
clatter on typewriters with no keys,
walk the streets in the tiny hours
chalking neat kisses on strangers' doors.

The ghosts of Liverpool 8 are invisible
but their words are everywhere if you know where to look.

Kid Auto on the M25

It's 6.15 and the road's a car park,
same as yesterday, same as every day,
and I'm listening to traffic reports –
jack-knifed lorries, road works,
a tiger on the west-bound, rips
in the space/time continuum at Potters Bar,
and suddenly he's there, mopped locks
squeezed into a tipped hat, kicking his heels
in a baggy-arsed swagger, thumb in pocket
as he weaves between cars, twirling his cane,
striking matches on the seat of his pants,
drawing, cock-eyed, on his smouldering tab.

No-one else seems to notice,
eyes glued to cars in front,
fingers tapping steering wheels
as he executes the perfect pratfall,
stumbling over outsized shoes,
mugging to the speed cameras
before shuffling on. I watch him
growing smaller in the mirror, desperate
not to lose the receding form, until
he turns, tips me a flickering wink
of East End charm, and I leave the car door open
as I stumble, stiff-legged, after him.

No Smoke

Fire can't be trusted, its dark heart
dancing, read in charred papers,
scandals and lies, the smell of smoke,
broken promises and last year's
Christmas trees. See, there are words
drifting before your eyes, twisting
to what you want them to be: a promise,
a rumour, a prayer. Better to trust
air or water, better still,
earth. Deep below, a rumble.
Ignore it.

Armada

Upturned boats, soft planks
greening amongst reeds, beading
peeled and cracked, oars lost,
bob like helpless, legless beetles.

Only the sun is golden, glancing
from sodden wood, flood damaged,
left behind. Who once crewed
these cast-off barques? Where are they now?

Clouds gather, wreckers on the shore,
pirates of treasured days, plundering
light, gunning thunder, lightning
drawing its ragged cutlass tightly
to the throat of evening, cursing and spitting
as ghosts return to blackening helms.

Afterglow

Where are you? There
in the weeds, in the reeds
at the lip of the lake, babbling
like a smiling Ophelia, embracing
almond blossom, celandine.

The water is so clear
it's invisible beneath you,
flying, cotton-winged,
hair streaming above
sunken bullion koi.

This is how it should be:
air like new milk, splashing
ripples into upturned hands,
cold below and palms glowing.

Sleeping with Dragons

The island stands no fire, no venom,
its barbarous beasts banished – long ago
fled the fishes' road to land,
hid deep in caves, colonised cracks
between prayer and superstition.

                            Now,
here on the hill, I share my dreaming
with dragons' descendants – lizards, half-waking
beneath my bed: 'Dim the lights,'
they plead, 'don't answer the door.'

Falcon

I. THE GENESIS OF FALCON

By the time He had done chickens,
puffins, parrots, and everything else
He hadn't got round to naming,
He had the measure of creation
with His eyes shut: Health & Safety
had flown out of the window.

Cocky and careless, He scrabbled flight
into hard lines, stabbed neat feathers
into a frame stripped bare to electric flex,
soldered eyes like beacons flashing
warnings of height and death.

Perfection came easy: Bird rebooted
to ripping machine of beak and talons
gripping His wrist. He held it close,
kissed his creation, inspired it with steel,
darkness and plunging fire.

II. FLEDGLING

huddled
tight
afraid

hesitant
unfolding
wingspread

first
tentative
flight

soaring

III. FALCON EXPLAINS

You think you know me,
think I'm tamed. Wrong.
Even wrist-bound, I'm dangerous,
more than you could know.

Yes, I fly higher, plunge faster
than you can see, my arrival
heralded by blood and feathers,
the fluttering dead. But

anyone can fly. Just spread your wings,
flap them: there you go.
Look at Crow. Even Penguin
could do it if he wasn't so dumb.

No, it's when I'm still
that you should fear me,
for when I've nothing in my grasp
I have your whole world in my eye.

The Alchemist's Cat

The philosopher's unblinking stone, I am
sublime, my substance refined, distilled
to quintessence of silence, self-contained
in my crucible of inscrutable darkness, yet

I'm the movement you almost see, the shimmer
at the corner of your eye, the flood of shadow
beneath your feet, the quicksilver claw –
but when you look again, I am

elsewhere, transfixed, reading secrets
in blank air, staring beyond
human understanding. Eternal
youth? Watch me play. Seriously:

look and learn. I'd burn my books
if I were you, settle by the blaze,
curl, Ouroborian, and let firelight
transmute my amber eyes to gold.

Toad Stone

You reach deep
beneath cold

ripples, numb
hand grasping

a gold-eyed toad,
squat in sediment.

Your cold mouth
spits no poison,

this swallowed stone
no frog in your throat.

A Tiding of Magpies

One's for sorrow, but two is a different story,
chattering welcomes to the unexpected, high
on branch and gable, blood turning to wine
beneath tale-telling tongues. A brace of witchbirds
flying to the sun, peeling layers from onions
deep in ragged pockets: *I defy thee, I defy thee,*
but don't try me. Dress your best and come aboard,
I'll raise my hat, spit three times, and together
we'll ride to steal silver from the gallows.

The Ringmaster's Apprentice

At the first scent of autumn she pitched her tent,
unfurling her rags and her old colours,
her hand-me-down gauds staining your neat fields.

As sure as days grew shorter, she stretched
her threadbare canvas, hoisted flags,
erected cages away from the paths.
With pained and patient fingers she sewed
constellations of teardrop sequins
to snatch your eye from tell-tale holes.

For days you never saw her, working
somewhere inside, but you might have heard her
distantly humming fairground tunes.
Late at night you'd sometimes catch sight of her,
heavy pails in hands, staggering
to feed her hungry, restless beasts.

As leaves fell, the air grew hard,
choking on greasepaint, burnt sugar,
wood smoke, sweat and expectation.

Unsure on your own land, you approach,
raise a tattered flap and enter,
tentatively take your ringside seat
as she paces the perimeter of her silent circle
to no applause, no cheers, no roars,
no brassy fanfare or cymbals' clash.

Now spotlights converge, colours blending
to fringed white as she takes her place,
facing her audience of one, opening
her scarlet mouth as wide as a lion's,
her tongue a tightrope where promises dance
like careless acrobats falling into fire.

A Word to St George

You made me out of odds and ends
left over from the armoury; scraps,
malformed rejects, welded piecemeal
to something uncertain you labelled 'dragon',
part crocodile, part armadillo,
clanking and scratching, writhing outside
your city walls. You signed up kids
to kill me, stop me in my tracks;
callow would-be heroes who didn't
stand a chance. Because, you see,
as long as armour's forged in fire,
you'll always make monsters, so
stuff your sword down my gaping throat,
I'll always bite you back.

Moon Ballet

after Hannah Frank

Eyes closed, faces raised,
we arch in darkness, arms aloft
in warm midnight fields.

Moonrise: a smooth lycanthropy of senses
wheels our windmill arms, grinding
slow blackness to stardust.

Limbs move to leaf-song, laughter
of owl and hare, wing-beat, foot-beat,
dancing in Dervish dreams.

We spin like spilt-milk galaxies
splashed half way to heaven,
high in silver, smiling.

Amid the trees, gentle on grass,
we are wind and tangled hair
blowing purposefully wild.

Tomorrow we may turn wheels, pages,
new leaves. But now we turn
ourselves. This madness is divine.

In the Waiting Room

For what do we wait in this harsh light and music
of slowly turned pages? It is a matter of percentages
and public awareness, of chance to inevitability,
of cautious glances and furtive movements to nowhere.

And while we wait we fold our fears like cold
chips in old news, screwed into stories
too banal to read again, feeding on fevers,
feeling the weight swallowed, heavy and hard

in the pits of our stomachs. We wait with the pained pressure
of passing time, pressing and pulping us to paper.

Intensive Care

Family, friends and strangers sing
anxious songs in hospital corners,
ward off spectres, drip-feed dreams
deep into the hard veins of night
passengers. Off the rails, off
the clip-boarded chart, heart-stopping
monitors flatline, screening time
ticking silence between empty beds.

Listen: there are so many words
muffled beneath starched blankets,
like platform announcements echoing through stations
that closed long before we were born.
Lay your head carefully on the pillow –
feel the rumble down the vanishing tracks.

If I Were You

I have no voice for those lacking tongues,
swallowing bile and dust, winnowing
words for bread in arid streets,
gleaning junk and rumour, sifting lies
for dignity, harvesting death
or, at least, non-life,
bent in doorways, no longer dreaming,
nor singing, nor even mouthing words
like: *pity, love, please*.

I won't be their smooth-fingered ventriloquist,
jerk inert heads, clatter jaws,
lull words into mouths in feigned accents,
my furious hands caressing the rictus to mute invitation:
come and admire vicarious, undreamable
thrills, dine at the feast of untasting
tongues, devour the disenfranchised,
lick your lips and say: *how frightful*.

Dark words stain white pages,
self-gratifying and pornographic;
furtive Polaroids from back alleys
passed and pawed in exclusive clubs, greasy
thumbprints bruising self-regarding lips,
with poverty puppeted, brought to the banquet
bearing nothing to the table, swallowing shadows,
leaving only crumbs of darkness.

Behind the serpent chatter – silence,
endless silence, and I have no voice.

Arches

When I met him, trying to crawl
under the railway arches, he explained,
lucidly, about the leaves he'd cut
from that foreign plant in the botanical gardens
and how he'd be especially grateful
if I'd be so kind as to watch out
for the pixies who had pursued him since the theft.

We spoke for a while as he huffed and heaved,
tenaciously failing to make headway
beneath the dark arches, until,
I'll give it a break, he said, lying prone,
allowing the weight to rest on his shoulders,
closing his eyes. I left him to it.

A short while after, I heard he'd been arrested
robbing a chemist's but, having left town,
I never saw him again. Later,
I heard he'd died at twenty-five –
a stolen bike chased to blackness
beneath a motorway flyover, a spreading
pharmacopoeia staining the road,
struggling to reach that other side
he'd always sought and, once again,
failing.

Monument

We are all free, there are no slaves
in England, as we celebrate civilised centuries,
escaping the past we choose to forget.

We have broken chains of cause and effect,
snapped the links that chafed and bound
to the embarrassing empire we have left behind.

We are free to sip coffee, flown
from starving children, barefoot and beaten,
fingers deep in poisoned earth,

to linger on the gold, the fine jewel,
dragged from darkness by numb hands
rubbed raw on tightening bonds.

And over our cities, Victorian eyes
brood in senseless stone, proud
and blind to streets they built from blood

where painted girls in sweatshop clothes
trade their bodies for nothing with men
they don't understand. We are all free.

The Demolition Men 1960

after a photograph by Jimmy Forsyth

A yellowing photo shows ragged men
who smashed down walls and tore down time,
piled it high on the back of their truck.

They ripped up cobbles and toppled gaslamps,
heaped the debris higher, until
the truck was buried. Pausing for Woodbines

they eyed the sky, featureless and grey,
took its measure, swung their picks,
drew it down upon their heads.

Buried beneath concrete, tarmac and traffic,
we never saw their like again
as, high in the vivid sky, appeared

The Beatles, waving from a submarine
the mellow tone of the endless sun
that warmed the 60s on colour TV.

A Rock'n'Roll Tour of Plymouth

We'll start with the obvious: here
ELP played their first gig, before the Isle of Wight,
were banned for life for damaging a tapestry
with an overenthusiastically flung dagger.

And this is where The Beatles played
two shows on the same day. Before my time,
though girls still screamed when they ran *Hard Day's Night*.
And *Summer Holiday*, come to think of it.

Before they built the mall, here was the club
where the Pistols played as a mystery band,
posters bearing nothing but a question mark
signalling to the drainpiped cognoscenti.

Somewhere near Toys 'R' Us, as I recall,
the post-Beeching arches once crumbled
onto the best selection of second-hand guitars
this side of Bristol. No questions asked.

Where the flats are now, or there on the wasteland,
amongst the Dickensian curiosities and porn mags,
a dank shop sold scuffed vinyl that smelled of damp,
by Germans and Italians your mates hadn't even heard of.

Probably in this garage, or maybe that church hall,
we played our first gig, drunk and out of tune,
practically cleared the place, drank more
and felt like we could conquer the world.

And just over there, past the houses,
is everything else: all the music in the world.
There we go, Blakey'd platforms sparking on cobbles,
hand-sewn flares flapping in the rock'n'roll night.

Vinyl Junkie

It begins like this: a ritual opening,
thumbnail-slit cellophane, chemical tang
inhaled deep, a fuzzy static buzz
bristling arm hairs, teasing the pulse
to pump a little faster. Always
like the first time: mouth dry
at the soft unsleeving, naked lines
dizzying to catch the track of ex-
pectation.
    The needle bites:
a soft, sharp caress that stops
time to muted white noise, dull
tom-tom heartbeats, the ice-crack
of not-quite-silence scratching awake
the kundalini serpent that swallows
180 grams, black and pure, straight
to the synapse.
    Here it comes.

Bound for Glory

Cheap guitar slung in the rack –
no case, I'm travelling light.
Tonight I'll party at the end of a line
drawn by the hand of Casey Jones,
from Rock Island, through the Cumberland Gap,
San Fernando – tons of steel
kicking up the dusty old dust
from back pocket paperbacks, thumbed
like goldrush maps: X marks the dream.

Blues harp brakes squeal,
the steaming engine shakes off rain
like an old dog settling for the night
as, in the scattered small-town lights,
the ghost of Woody Guthrie pauses,
raises his whisky and smiles, turns back
to his tall stories as I pick up speed,
rattling down rails with my cheap guitar,
bound for Glory (changing at Crewe).

Elvis Lives Next Door

His hair's now white, cropped close,
he sports a neat goatee,
wears loose trousers in the garden,
a sweater that's thin at the elbows,
sometimes he smokes a pipe.
He's lost a lot of weight,
looks better for it, more healthy
than he did in the seventies. Now,
in *his* seventies, he smiles
rather than sneers, his lip
curling to a private joke.

He keeps himself to himself,
though is friendly enough, a regular
in the pub on a Friday night.
I didn't suspect it was him
until once, after a couple of Guinnesses,
he got up for the karaoke,
swivelling his replacement hip
as he hollered 'Jailhouse Rock',
amazed us all. Later
in the gents, I had to ask:
'Are you…?' I let the question hang.

He turned from the sink, fixed me
with his steady blue eyes,
shrugged his shoulders and said:
'uh-huh.'

Bad

From Ben to Billie Jean and beyond,
he passed me by. Messianic videos,
statues almost the size of an ego,
even Jarvis Cocker's arse –
somehow I hardly even noticed.

Trial by tabloid I couldn't ignore
completely, but apart from a sly dig
in a Richard Thompson song, nothing
crossed the rainbow bridge from his Neverland world.

So, when he died, I ignored the tributes,
skipped the scandals in the morning papers
and turned to the real news. But,
there was a photo: a young boy,
maybe twelve, maybe younger,
big eyed, black skinned,
before hysteria, before surgery,
before accusations. Smiling.

And I remembered a song, trite and pure,
about young love and sharing the world,
from back in the day when I was young
and smiling and wanted to be a star.

And I missed the details, and I don't know
who was right and who was lying,
but I thought about that young boy singing
that simple song, and all the damage
and all the pain that followed. And what I did know
was that I was glad I wasn't him. And sad
that he never had the chance to be anyone else.

Asylum

We walk in soft shoes on fragile floors,
doors locked to left and right.

Embarrassed eyes avoid each other
and ourselves. There are no mirrors.

Empty shelves, warped with the weight
of absence, warn: *do not touch.*

Sometimes we recall who left us here,
how long ago and why. But

it's better to forget, to accept our state,
repeat the mantra: *we are safe here*,

surrounded by stained glass birds,
watched over by a clock with no hands.

Statte Station

after Paul Delvaux

Sky hangs low, slapped and silver.
At the line's end, phantoms fade to bones
in the last car, cradling your death
through all your nights' journeys.

By the light of dark lanterns, mermaids wait,
tails concealed beneath neat dresses, perfect
hair framing sad faces. Dreams of the deep
seep through soft, grey carpets.

The seated widow slowly combs her hair
between night and mirrors, bare
white legs defined hard beneath weeds,
black garments pinned to the floor.

Within a frame of scented lamps,
a discarded shift blisters to life, its shadows
mistaken, as a fugitive moon catches in branches,
reflected in the glow of surrounding seas.

while we slept

and while we slept, the sea grew hard,
grey under black sky, salt
souring with metal, abrading the shore

and, before morning, we may have heard
(but can't be sure) a cry, or thunder,
or a lone bird, but did not wake

and the sea rose, sluggish and warm
like blood, its slow pulse lulling
our indolent sleep, deeper and deeper

and deeper still, until we swam
submerged in dark magnetic depths,
dreaming of waking up and glowing.

Passing Over

And when you reach the border that isn't on the map,
get dressed as soon as the labourers break into your compartment.
And when they start removing the floor panels, try not to meet
their eyes. And when the smart man asks you to fill in forms
in languages you do not recognise, as a young boy
in a crisp uniform crawls through the luggage racks,
try not to dwell on the way you skimmed the small print
in guidebooks you should have read more closely. And though,
when they lead you silently onto the foggy sidings at 3am,
you will inevitably recall cheap paperbacks and grainy movies,
try instead to consider what you truly believe, and whether or not
it is what they also believe. And, most importantly,
when the elderly woman with too much makeup,
sitting stiffly in the over-lit, overheated hut – the only person
who smiles and speaks your native tongue – makes her simple demand,
make sure you are carrying exactly what she asks for.